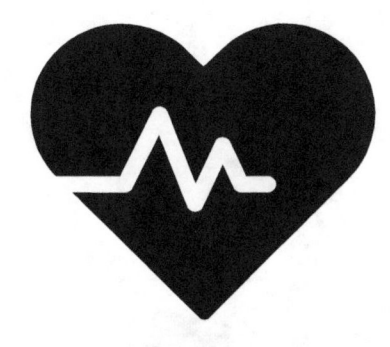

WORKOUT
Log Book

NAME: _____

PHONE: _____

WORKOUT *Log*

DATE: S M T W T F S

INTENSITY

TODAY'S GOAL

STARTING WEIGHT

GOAL WEIGHT

CURRENT WEIGHT

WATER

💧💧💧💧💧💧💧💧

WEIGHTS

EXERCISE	WEIGHT	SETS	REPS	TIME

CARDIO

EXERCISE	DISTANCE	SETS	REPS	TIME

NOTES

WORKOUT *Log*

DATE: S M T W T F S   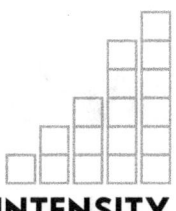 INTENSITY

TODAY'S GOAL

STARTING WEIGHT

GOAL WEIGHT

CURRENT WEIGHT

WATER ○○○○○○○○

WEIGHTS

EXERCISE	WEIGHT	SETS	REPS	TIME

CARDIO

EXERCISE	DISTANCE	SETS	REPS	TIME

NOTES

WORKOUT *Log*

DATE: S M T W T F S   **INTENSITY**

TODAY'S GOAL

STARTING WEIGHT

GOAL WEIGHT

CURRENT WEIGHT

WATER

💧💧💧💧💧💧💧💧

WEIGHTS

EXERCISE	WEIGHT	SETS	REPS	TIME

CARDIO

EXERCISE	DISTANCE	SETS	REPS	TIME

NOTES

WORKOUT *Log*

DATE: S M T W T F S

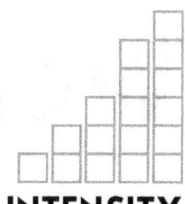

INTENSITY

TODAY'S GOAL

_____
_____
_____

STARTING WEIGHT _____
GOAL WEIGHT _____
CURRENT WEIGHT _____
WATER
◇ ◇ ◇ ◇ ◇ ◇ ◇ ◇

WEIGHTS

EXERCISE	WEIGHT	SETS	REPS	TIME

CARDIO

EXERCISE	DISTANCE	SETS	REPS	TIME

NOTES

_____
_____

WORKOUT *Log*

DATE: **S M T W T F S**

INTENSITY

TODAY'S GOAL

STARTING WEIGHT

GOAL WEIGHT

CURRENT WEIGHT

WATER
◯ ◯ ◯ ◯ ◯ ◯ ◯ ◯

WEIGHTS

EXERCISE	WEIGHT	SETS	REPS	TIME

CARDIO

EXERCISE	DISTANCE	SETS	REPS	TIME

NOTES

WORKOUT *Log*

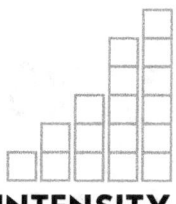

DATE: **S M T W T F S**   **INTENSITY**

TODAY'S GOAL

STARTING WEIGHT

GOAL WEIGHT

CURRENT WEIGHT

WATER

 ◊ ◊ ◊ ◊ ◊ ◊ ◊ ◊

WEIGHTS

EXERCISE	WEIGHT	SETS	REPS	TIME

CARDIO

EXERCISE	DISTANCE	SETS	REPS	TIME

NOTES

WORKOUT *Log*

DATE: S M T W T F S   **INTENSITY**

TODAY'S GOAL

STARTING WEIGHT
GOAL WEIGHT
CURRENT WEIGHT
WATER
💧💧💧💧💧💧💧💧

WEIGHTS

EXERCISE	WEIGHT	SETS	REPS	TIME

CARDIO

EXERCISE	DISTANCE	SETS	REPS	TIME

NOTES

WORKOUT *Log*

DATE: S M T W T F S

INTENSITY

TODAY'S GOAL

STARTING WEIGHT

GOAL WEIGHT

CURRENT WEIGHT

WATER
○ ○ ○ ○ ○ ○ ○ ○

WEIGHTS

EXERCISE	WEIGHT	SETS	REPS	TIME

CARDIO

EXERCISE	DISTANCE	SETS	REPS	TIME

NOTES

WORKOUT *Log*

DATE: S M T W T F S   INTENSITY

TODAY'S GOAL

STARTING WEIGHT

GOAL WEIGHT

CURRENT WEIGHT

WATER ⬭⬭⬭⬭⬭⬭⬭⬭

WEIGHTS

EXERCISE	WEIGHT	SETS	REPS	TIME

CARDIO

EXERCISE	DISTANCE	SETS	REPS	TIME

NOTES

WORKOUT *Log*

DATE: S M T W T F S

INTENSITY

TODAY'S GOAL

STARTING WEIGHT

GOAL WEIGHT

CURRENT WEIGHT

WATER

◯ ◯ ◯ ◯ ◯ ◯ ◯ ◯

WEIGHTS

EXERCISE	WEIGHT	SETS	REPS	TIME

CARDIO

EXERCISE	DISTANCE	SETS	REPS	TIME

NOTES

WORKOUT *Log*

DATE: S M T W T F S

INTENSITY

TODAY'S GOAL

STARTING WEIGHT
GOAL WEIGHT
CURRENT WEIGHT
WATER
 ⬭⬭⬭⬭⬭⬭⬭⬭

WEIGHTS

EXERCISE	WEIGHT	SETS	REPS	TIME

CARDIO

EXERCISE	DISTANCE	SETS	REPS	TIME

NOTES

WORKOUT *Log*

INTENSITY

DATE: S M T W T F S

TODAY'S GOAL

STARTING WEIGHT

GOAL WEIGHT

CURRENT WEIGHT

WATER
💧💧💧💧💧💧💧💧

WEIGHTS

EXERCISE	WEIGHT	SETS	REPS	TIME

CARDIO

EXERCISE	DISTANCE	SETS	REPS	TIME

NOTES

WORKOUT *Log*

DATE: S M T W T F S   **INTENSITY**

TODAY'S GOAL

STARTING WEIGHT

GOAL WEIGHT

CURRENT WEIGHT

WATER
💧💧💧💧💧💧💧💧

WEIGHTS

EXERCISE	WEIGHT	SETS	REPS	TIME

CARDIO

EXERCISE	DISTANCE	SETS	REPS	TIME

NOTES

WORKOUT *Log*

DATE: _____ S M T W T F S

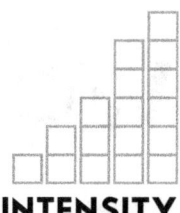

INTENSITY

TODAY'S GOAL

_____
_____
_____

STARTING WEIGHT _____
GOAL WEIGHT _____
CURRENT WEIGHT _____
WATER
◇ ◇ ◇ ◇ ◇ ◇ ◇ ◇

WEIGHTS

EXERCISE	WEIGHT	SETS	REPS	TIME

CARDIO

EXERCISE	DISTANCE	SETS	REPS	TIME

NOTES

_____
_____

WORKOUT *Log*

DATE: S M T W T F S   **INTENSITY**

TODAY'S GOAL

STARTING WEIGHT
GOAL WEIGHT
CURRENT WEIGHT
WATER
◊ ◊ ◊ ◊ ◊ ◊ ◊ ◊

WEIGHTS

EXERCISE	WEIGHT	SETS	REPS	TIME

CARDIO

EXERCISE	DISTANCE	SETS	REPS	TIME

NOTES

WORKOUT *Log*

DATE: S M T W T F S

INTENSITY

TODAY'S GOAL

STARTING WEIGHT

GOAL WEIGHT

CURRENT WEIGHT

WATER

WEIGHTS

EXERCISE	WEIGHT	SETS	REPS	TIME

CARDIO

EXERCISE	DISTANCE	SETS	REPS	TIME

NOTES

WORKOUT *Log*

DATE: S M T W T F S   INTENSITY

TODAY'S GOAL

STARTING WEIGHT

GOAL WEIGHT

CURRENT WEIGHT

WATER

WEIGHTS

EXERCISE	WEIGHT	SETS	REPS	TIME

CARDIO

EXERCISE	DISTANCE	SETS	REPS	TIME

NOTES

WORKOUT *Log*

DATE: S M T W T F S

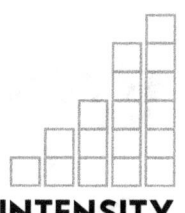

INTENSITY

TODAY'S GOAL

STARTING WEIGHT
GOAL WEIGHT
CURRENT WEIGHT
WATER
💧💧💧💧💧💧💧💧

WEIGHTS

EXERCISE	WEIGHT	SETS	REPS	TIME

CARDIO

EXERCISE	DISTANCE	SETS	REPS	TIME

NOTES

WORKOUT *Log*

DATE: S M T W T F S   **INTENSITY**

TODAY'S GOAL

STARTING WEIGHT

GOAL WEIGHT

CURRENT WEIGHT

WATER

WEIGHTS

EXERCISE	WEIGHT	SETS	REPS	TIME

CARDIO

EXERCISE	DISTANCE	SETS	REPS	TIME

NOTES

WORKOUT *Log*

DATE: S M T W T F S   **INTENSITY**

TODAY'S GOAL

STARTING WEIGHT

GOAL WEIGHT

CURRENT WEIGHT

WATER

WEIGHTS

EXERCISE	WEIGHT	SETS	REPS	TIME

CARDIO

EXERCISE	DISTANCE	SETS	REPS	TIME

NOTES

WORKOUT *Log*

DATE: **S M T W T F S**   **INTENSITY**

TODAY'S GOAL

STARTING WEIGHT

GOAL WEIGHT

CURRENT WEIGHT

WATER ◇◇◇◇◇◇◇◇

WEIGHTS

EXERCISE	WEIGHT	SETS	REPS	TIME

CARDIO

EXERCISE	DISTANCE	SETS	REPS	TIME

NOTES

WORKOUT *Log*

DATE: S M T W T F S

INTENSITY

TODAY'S GOAL

STARTING WEIGHT
GOAL WEIGHT
CURRENT WEIGHT
WATER
🌢 🌢 🌢 🌢 🌢 🌢 🌢 🌢

WEIGHTS

EXERCISE	WEIGHT	SETS	REPS	TIME

CARDIO

EXERCISE	DISTANCE	SETS	REPS	TIME

NOTES

WORKOUT *Log*

DATE: _____ S M T W T F S

INTENSITY

TODAY'S GOAL
_____
_____
_____

STARTING WEIGHT _____
GOAL WEIGHT _____
CURRENT WEIGHT _____
WATER
○ ○ ○ ○ ○ ○ ○ ○

WEIGHTS

EXERCISE	WEIGHT	SETS	REPS	TIME

CARDIO

EXERCISE	DISTANCE	SETS	REPS	TIME

NOTES
_____
_____

WORKOUT *Log*

DATE: S M T W T F S **INTENSITY**

TODAY'S GOAL

STARTING WEIGHT
GOAL WEIGHT
CURRENT WEIGHT
WATER
◊ ◊ ◊ ◊ ◊ ◊ ◊ ◊

WEIGHTS

EXERCISE	WEIGHT	SETS	REPS	TIME

CARDIO

EXERCISE	DISTANCE	SETS	REPS	TIME

NOTES

WORKOUT *Log*

DATE: S M T W T F S

INTENSITY

TODAY'S GOAL

STARTING WEIGHT

GOAL WEIGHT

CURRENT WEIGHT

WATER

WEIGHTS

EXERCISE	WEIGHT	SETS	REPS	TIME

CARDIO

EXERCISE	DISTANCE	SETS	REPS	TIME

NOTES

WORKOUT *Log*

DATE: S M T W T F S

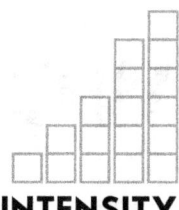

INTENSITY

TODAY'S GOAL

_____
_____
_____

STARTING WEIGHT _____
GOAL WEIGHT _____
CURRENT WEIGHT _____
WATER
○ ○ ○ ○ ○ ○ ○ ○

WEIGHTS

EXERCISE	WEIGHT	SETS	REPS	TIME

CARDIO

EXERCISE	DISTANCE	SETS	REPS	TIME

NOTES

_____
_____

WORKOUT *Log*

DATE: S M T W T F S   **INTENSITY**

TODAY'S GOAL

STARTING WEIGHT

GOAL WEIGHT

CURRENT WEIGHT

WATER
◊ ◊ ◊ ◊ ◊ ◊ ◊ ◊

WEIGHTS

EXERCISE	WEIGHT	SETS	REPS	TIME

CARDIO

EXERCISE	DISTANCE	SETS	REPS	TIME

NOTES

WORKOUT *Log*

DATE: S M T W T F S

INTENSITY

TODAY'S GOAL

STARTING WEIGHT

GOAL WEIGHT

CURRENT WEIGHT

WATER

WEIGHTS

EXERCISE	WEIGHT	SETS	REPS	TIME

CARDIO

EXERCISE	DISTANCE	SETS	REPS	TIME

NOTES

WORKOUT *Log*

DATE: S M T W T F S   **INTENSITY**

TODAY'S GOAL

STARTING WEIGHT

GOAL WEIGHT

CURRENT WEIGHT

WATER
○ ○ ○ ○ ○ ○ ○ ○

WEIGHTS

EXERCISE	WEIGHT	SETS	REPS	TIME

CARDIO

EXERCISE	DISTANCE	SETS	REPS	TIME

NOTES

WORKOUT *Log*

DATE: S M T W T F S

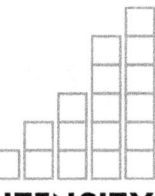
INTENSITY

TODAY'S GOAL

_____
_____
_____

STARTING WEIGHT _____
GOAL WEIGHT _____
CURRENT WEIGHT _____
WATER
○ ○ ○ ○ ○ ○ ○ ○

WEIGHTS

EXERCISE	WEIGHT	SETS	REPS	TIME

CARDIO

EXERCISE	DISTANCE	SETS	REPS	TIME

NOTES

_____
_____

WORKOUT *Log*

DATE: S M T W T F S   **INTENSITY**

TODAY'S GOAL

STARTING WEIGHT
GOAL WEIGHT
CURRENT WEIGHT
WATER
💧💧💧💧💧💧💧💧

WEIGHTS

EXERCISE	WEIGHT	SETS	REPS	TIME

CARDIO

EXERCISE	DISTANCE	SETS	REPS	TIME

NOTES

WORKOUT *Log*

DATE: _____   S M T W T F S

INTENSITY

TODAY'S GOAL

_____
_____
_____

STARTING WEIGHT _____
GOAL WEIGHT _____
CURRENT WEIGHT _____
WATER
○ ○ ○ ○ ○ ○ ○ ○

WEIGHTS

EXERCISE	WEIGHT	SETS	REPS	TIME

CARDIO

EXERCISE	DISTANCE	SETS	REPS	TIME

NOTES

_____
_____

WORKOUT *Log*

DATE: S M T W T F S   **INTENSITY**

TODAY'S GOAL

STARTING WEIGHT

GOAL WEIGHT

CURRENT WEIGHT

WATER

WEIGHTS

EXERCISE	WEIGHT	SETS	REPS	TIME

CARDIO

EXERCISE	DISTANCE	SETS	REPS	TIME

NOTES

WORKOUT *Log*

DATE: S M T W T F S

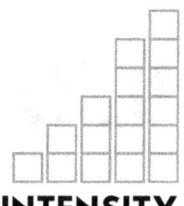

INTENSITY

TODAY'S GOAL

STARTING WEIGHT

GOAL WEIGHT

CURRENT WEIGHT

WATER
○ ○ ○ ○ ○ ○ ○ ○

WEIGHTS

EXERCISE	WEIGHT	SETS	REPS	TIME

CARDIO

EXERCISE	DISTANCE	SETS	REPS	TIME

NOTES

WORKOUT *Log*

DATE: S M T W T F S   **INTENSITY**

TODAY'S GOAL

STARTING WEIGHT

GOAL WEIGHT

CURRENT WEIGHT

WATER

WEIGHTS

EXERCISE	WEIGHT	SETS	REPS	TIME

CARDIO

EXERCISE	DISTANCE	SETS	REPS	TIME

NOTES

WORKOUT *Log*

DATE: S M T W T F S   **INTENSITY**

TODAY'S GOAL

STARTING WEIGHT

GOAL WEIGHT

CURRENT WEIGHT

WATER

WEIGHTS

EXERCISE	WEIGHT	SETS	REPS	TIME

CARDIO

EXERCISE	DISTANCE	SETS	REPS	TIME

NOTES

WORKOUT *Log*

DATE: **S M T W T F S**

INTENSITY

TODAY'S GOAL

STARTING WEIGHT
GOAL WEIGHT
CURRENT WEIGHT
WATER
💧💧💧💧💧💧💧💧

WEIGHTS

EXERCISE	WEIGHT	SETS	REPS	TIME

CARDIO

EXERCISE	DISTANCE	SETS	REPS	TIME

NOTES

WORKOUT *Log*

DATE: S M T W T F S   **INTENSITY**

TODAY'S GOAL

STARTING WEIGHT

GOAL WEIGHT

CURRENT WEIGHT

WATER

WEIGHTS

EXERCISE	WEIGHT	SETS	REPS	TIME

CARDIO

EXERCISE	DISTANCE	SETS	REPS	TIME

NOTES

WORKOUT *Log*

DATE: S M T W T F S

INTENSITY

TODAY'S GOAL

STARTING WEIGHT

GOAL WEIGHT

CURRENT WEIGHT

WATER
○ ○ ○ ○ ○ ○ ○ ○

WEIGHTS

EXERCISE	WEIGHT	SETS	REPS	TIME

CARDIO

EXERCISE	DISTANCE	SETS	REPS	TIME

NOTES

WORKOUT *Log*

DATE: S M T W T F S   **INTENSITY**

TODAY'S GOAL

STARTING WEIGHT
GOAL WEIGHT
CURRENT WEIGHT
WATER
💧💧💧💧💧💧💧💧

WEIGHTS

EXERCISE	WEIGHT	SETS	REPS	TIME

CARDIO

EXERCISE	DISTANCE	SETS	REPS	TIME

NOTES

WORKOUT *Log*

DATE: S M T W T F S   **INTENSITY**

TODAY'S GOAL

STARTING WEIGHT

GOAL WEIGHT

CURRENT WEIGHT

WATER
⬭ ⬭ ⬭ ⬭ ⬭ ⬭ ⬭ ⬭

WEIGHTS

EXERCISE	WEIGHT	SETS	REPS	TIME

CARDIO

EXERCISE	DISTANCE	SETS	REPS	TIME

NOTES

WORKOUT *Log*

DATE: S M T W T F S   **INTENSITY**

TODAY'S GOAL

STARTING WEIGHT

GOAL WEIGHT

CURRENT WEIGHT

WATER

WEIGHTS

EXERCISE	WEIGHT	SETS	REPS	TIME

CARDIO

EXERCISE	DISTANCE	SETS	REPS	TIME

NOTES

WORKOUT *Log*

DATE: S M T W T F S   **INTENSITY**

TODAY'S GOAL

STARTING WEIGHT

GOAL WEIGHT

CURRENT WEIGHT

WATER

◯ ◯ ◯ ◯ ◯ ◯ ◯ ◯

WEIGHTS

EXERCISE	WEIGHT	SETS	REPS	TIME

CARDIO

EXERCISE	DISTANCE	SETS	REPS	TIME

NOTES

WORKOUT *Log*

DATE: S M T W T F S   **INTENSITY**

TODAY'S GOAL

STARTING WEIGHT

GOAL WEIGHT

CURRENT WEIGHT

WATER

WEIGHTS

EXERCISE	WEIGHT	SETS	REPS	TIME

CARDIO

EXERCISE	DISTANCE	SETS	REPS	TIME

NOTES

WORKOUT *Log*

DATE: **S M T W T F S**   **INTENSITY**

TODAY'S GOAL

STARTING WEIGHT

GOAL WEIGHT

CURRENT WEIGHT

WATER
◊ ◊ ◊ ◊ ◊ ◊ ◊ ◊

WEIGHTS

EXERCISE	WEIGHT	SETS	REPS	TIME

CARDIO

EXERCISE	DISTANCE	SETS	REPS	TIME

NOTES

WORKOUT *Log*

DATE: S M T W T F S   **INTENSITY**

TODAY'S GOAL

STARTING WEIGHT

GOAL WEIGHT

CURRENT WEIGHT

WATER

💧💧💧💧💧💧💧💧

WEIGHTS

EXERCISE	WEIGHT	SETS	REPS	TIME

CARDIO

EXERCISE	DISTANCE	SETS	REPS	TIME

NOTES

WORKOUT *Log*

DATE: S M T W T F S   **INTENSITY**

TODAY'S GOAL

STARTING WEIGHT

GOAL WEIGHT

CURRENT WEIGHT

WATER
💧💧💧💧💧💧💧💧

WEIGHTS

EXERCISE	WEIGHT	SETS	REPS	TIME

CARDIO

EXERCISE	DISTANCE	SETS	REPS	TIME

NOTES

WORKOUT *Log*

DATE: S M T W T F S   **INTENSITY**

TODAY'S GOAL

STARTING WEIGHT
GOAL WEIGHT
CURRENT WEIGHT
WATER
◊ ◊ ◊ ◊ ◊ ◊ ◊ ◊

WEIGHTS

EXERCISE	WEIGHT	SETS	REPS	TIME

CARDIO

EXERCISE	DISTANCE	SETS	REPS	TIME

NOTES

WORKOUT *Log*

DATE: **S M T W T F S**   **INTENSITY**

TODAY'S GOAL

STARTING WEIGHT

GOAL WEIGHT

CURRENT WEIGHT

WATER

WEIGHTS

EXERCISE	WEIGHT	SETS	REPS	TIME

CARDIO

EXERCISE	DISTANCE	SETS	REPS	TIME

NOTES

WORKOUT *Log*

DATE: **S M T W T F S** **INTENSITY**

TODAY'S GOAL

STARTING WEIGHT
GOAL WEIGHT
CURRENT WEIGHT
WATER

WEIGHTS

EXERCISE	WEIGHT	SETS	REPS	TIME

CARDIO

EXERCISE	DISTANCE	SETS	REPS	TIME

NOTES

WORKOUT *Log*

DATE: **S M T W T F S**   **INTENSITY**

TODAY'S GOAL

STARTING WEIGHT

GOAL WEIGHT

CURRENT WEIGHT

WATER
○ ○ ○ ○ ○ ○ ○ ○

WEIGHTS

EXERCISE	WEIGHT	SETS	REPS	TIME

CARDIO

EXERCISE	DISTANCE	SETS	REPS	TIME

NOTES

WORKOUT *Log*

DATE: S M T W T F S

INTENSITY

TODAY'S GOAL

STARTING WEIGHT

GOAL WEIGHT

CURRENT WEIGHT

WATER

💧💧💧💧💧💧💧💧

WEIGHTS

EXERCISE	WEIGHT	SETS	REPS	TIME

CARDIO

EXERCISE	DISTANCE	SETS	REPS	TIME

NOTES

WORKOUT *Log*

DATE: **S M T W T F S**   **INTENSITY**

TODAY'S GOAL

STARTING WEIGHT

GOAL WEIGHT

CURRENT WEIGHT

WATER

WEIGHTS

EXERCISE	WEIGHT	SETS	REPS	TIME

CARDIO

EXERCISE	DISTANCE	SETS	REPS	TIME

NOTES

WORKOUT *Log*

DATE: S M T W T F S   **INTENSITY**

TODAY'S GOAL

STARTING WEIGHT

GOAL WEIGHT

CURRENT WEIGHT

WATER

WEIGHTS

EXERCISE	WEIGHT	SETS	REPS	TIME

CARDIO

EXERCISE	DISTANCE	SETS	REPS	TIME

NOTES

WORKOUT *Log*

DATE: S M T W T F S   **INTENSITY**

TODAY'S GOAL

STARTING WEIGHT

GOAL WEIGHT

CURRENT WEIGHT

WATER

◯ ◯ ◯ ◯ ◯ ◯ ◯ ◯

WEIGHTS

EXERCISE	WEIGHT	SETS	REPS	TIME

CARDIO

EXERCISE	DISTANCE	SETS	REPS	TIME

NOTES

_# WORKOUT *Log*

DATE: S M T W T F S INTENSITY

TODAY'S GOAL

STARTING WEIGHT
GOAL WEIGHT
CURRENT WEIGHT
WATER
💧💧💧💧💧💧💧💧

WEIGHTS

EXERCISE | WEIGHT | SETS | REPS | TIME

CARDIO

EXERCISE | DISTANCE | SETS | REPS | TIME

NOTES

WORKOUT *Log*

DATE: **S M T W T F S**   **INTENSITY**

TODAY'S GOAL

STARTING WEIGHT

GOAL WEIGHT

CURRENT WEIGHT

WATER

WEIGHTS

EXERCISE	WEIGHT	SETS	REPS	TIME

CARDIO

EXERCISE	DISTANCE	SETS	REPS	TIME

NOTES

WORKOUT *Log*

DATE: S M T W T F S

INTENSITY

TODAY'S GOAL

STARTING WEIGHT
GOAL WEIGHT
CURRENT WEIGHT
WATER
○ ○ ○ ○ ○ ○ ○ ○

WEIGHTS

EXERCISE	WEIGHT	SETS	REPS	TIME

CARDIO

EXERCISE	DISTANCE	SETS	REPS	TIME

NOTES

WORKOUT *Log*

DATE: S M T W T F S   **INTENSITY**

TODAY'S GOAL

STARTING WEIGHT

GOAL WEIGHT

CURRENT WEIGHT

WATER
💧💧💧💧💧💧💧💧

WEIGHTS

EXERCISE	WEIGHT	SETS	REPS	TIME

CARDIO

EXERCISE	DISTANCE	SETS	REPS	TIME

NOTES

WORKOUT *Log*

DATE: **S M T W T F S**   **INTENSITY**

TODAY'S GOAL

STARTING WEIGHT

GOAL WEIGHT

CURRENT WEIGHT

WATER

◊ ◊ ◊ ◊ ◊ ◊ ◊ ◊

WEIGHTS

EXERCISE	WEIGHT	SETS	REPS	TIME

CARDIO

EXERCISE	DISTANCE	SETS	REPS	TIME

NOTES

WORKOUT *Log*

DATE: **S M T W T F S**   **INTENSITY**

TODAY'S GOAL

STARTING WEIGHT

GOAL WEIGHT

CURRENT WEIGHT

WATER

WEIGHTS

EXERCISE	WEIGHT	SETS	REPS	TIME

CARDIO

EXERCISE	DISTANCE	SETS	REPS	TIME

NOTES

WORKOUT *Log*

DATE: S M T W T F S   **INTENSITY**

TODAY'S GOAL

STARTING WEIGHT

GOAL WEIGHT

CURRENT WEIGHT

WATER

○ ○ ○ ○ ○ ○ ○ ○

WEIGHTS

EXERCISE	WEIGHT	SETS	REPS	TIME

CARDIO

EXERCISE	DISTANCE	SETS	REPS	TIME

NOTES

WORKOUT *Log*

DATE: S M T W T F S   **INTENSITY**

TODAY'S GOAL

STARTING WEIGHT

GOAL WEIGHT

CURRENT WEIGHT

WATER

WEIGHTS

EXERCISE	WEIGHT	SETS	REPS	TIME

CARDIO

EXERCISE	DISTANCE	SETS	REPS	TIME

NOTES

WORKOUT *Log*

DATE: S M T W T F S   **INTENSITY**

TODAY'S GOAL

STARTING WEIGHT

GOAL WEIGHT

CURRENT WEIGHT

WATER
○ ○ ○ ○ ○ ○ ○ ○

WEIGHTS

EXERCISE	WEIGHT	SETS	REPS	TIME

CARDIO

EXERCISE	DISTANCE	SETS	REPS	TIME

NOTES

WORKOUT *Log*

DATE: **S M T W T F S**   **INTENSITY**

TODAY'S GOAL

STARTING WEIGHT

GOAL WEIGHT

CURRENT WEIGHT

WATER

WEIGHTS

EXERCISE	WEIGHT	SETS	REPS	TIME

CARDIO

EXERCISE	DISTANCE	SETS	REPS	TIME

NOTES

WORKOUT *Log*

DATE: S M T W T F S

INTENSITY

TODAY'S GOAL

_____
_____

STARTING WEIGHT _____
GOAL WEIGHT _____
CURRENT WEIGHT _____
WATER
◯ ◯ ◯ ◯ ◯ ◯ ◯ ◯

WEIGHTS

EXERCISE	WEIGHT	SETS	REPS	TIME

CARDIO

EXERCISE	DISTANCE	SETS	REPS	TIME

NOTES

_____
_____

WORKOUT *Log*

DATE: S M T W T F S   **INTENSITY**

TODAY'S GOAL

STARTING WEIGHT

GOAL WEIGHT

CURRENT WEIGHT

WATER

WEIGHTS

EXERCISE   WEIGHT   SETS   REPS   TIME

CARDIO

EXERCISE   DISTANCE   SETS   REPS   TIME

NOTES

WORKOUT *Log*

DATE: S M T W T F S   **INTENSITY**

TODAY'S GOAL

STARTING WEIGHT

GOAL WEIGHT

CURRENT WEIGHT

WATER

WEIGHTS

EXERCISE	WEIGHT	SETS	REPS	TIME

CARDIO

EXERCISE	DISTANCE	SETS	REPS	TIME

NOTES

WORKOUT *Log*

DATE: S M T W T F S   **INTENSITY**

TODAY'S GOAL

STARTING WEIGHT

GOAL WEIGHT

CURRENT WEIGHT

WATER
〇〇〇〇〇〇〇〇

WEIGHTS

EXERCISE	WEIGHT	SETS	REPS	TIME

CARDIO

EXERCISE	DISTANCE	SETS	REPS	TIME

NOTES

WORKOUT *Log*

DATE: **S M T W T F S**   **INTENSITY**

TODAY'S GOAL

STARTING WEIGHT

GOAL WEIGHT

CURRENT WEIGHT

WATER
○ ○ ○ ○ ○ ○ ○ ○

WEIGHTS

EXERCISE	WEIGHT	SETS	REPS	TIME

CARDIO

EXERCISE	DISTANCE	SETS	REPS	TIME

NOTES

WORKOUT *Log*

DATE: S M T W T F S   **INTENSITY**

TODAY'S GOAL

STARTING WEIGHT

GOAL WEIGHT

CURRENT WEIGHT

WATER

WEIGHTS

EXERCISE	WEIGHT	SETS	REPS	TIME

CARDIO

EXERCISE	DISTANCE	SETS	REPS	TIME

NOTES

WORKOUT *Log*

DATE: S M T W T F S   **INTENSITY**

TODAY'S GOAL

STARTING WEIGHT
GOAL WEIGHT
CURRENT WEIGHT
WATER
💧💧💧💧💧💧💧💧

WEIGHTS

EXERCISE	WEIGHT	SETS	REPS	TIME

CARDIO

EXERCISE	DISTANCE	SETS	REPS	TIME

NOTES

WORKOUT *Log*

DATE: S M T W T F S   INTENSITY

TODAY'S GOAL

STARTING WEIGHT

GOAL WEIGHT

CURRENT WEIGHT

WATER
○ ○ ○ ○ ○ ○ ○ ○

WEIGHTS

EXERCISE	WEIGHT	SETS	REPS	TIME

CARDIO

EXERCISE	DISTANCE	SETS	REPS	TIME

NOTES

WORKOUT *Log*

DATE: S M T W T F S   **INTENSITY**

TODAY'S GOAL

STARTING WEIGHT
GOAL WEIGHT
CURRENT WEIGHT
WATER
◊ ◊ ◊ ◊ ◊ ◊ ◊ ◊

WEIGHTS

EXERCISE	WEIGHT	SETS	REPS	TIME

CARDIO

EXERCISE	DISTANCE	SETS	REPS	TIME

NOTES

WORKOUT *Log*

DATE: S M T W T F S

INTENSITY

TODAY'S GOAL

STARTING WEIGHT
GOAL WEIGHT
CURRENT WEIGHT
WATER

WEIGHTS

EXERCISE   WEIGHT   SETS   REPS   TIME

CARDIO

EXERCISE   DISTANCE   SETS   REPS   TIME

NOTES

WORKOUT *Log*

DATE: **S M T W T F S**   **INTENSITY**

TODAY'S GOAL

STARTING WEIGHT
GOAL WEIGHT
CURRENT WEIGHT
WATER
💧💧💧💧💧💧💧💧

WEIGHTS

EXERCISE	WEIGHT	SETS	REPS	TIME

CARDIO

EXERCISE	DISTANCE	SETS	REPS	TIME

NOTES

WORKOUT *Log*

DATE: S M T W T F S   **INTENSITY**

TODAY'S GOAL

STARTING WEIGHT

GOAL WEIGHT

CURRENT WEIGHT

WATER
○ ○ ○ ○ ○ ○ ○ ○

WEIGHTS

EXERCISE	WEIGHT	SETS	REPS	TIME

CARDIO

EXERCISE	DISTANCE	SETS	REPS	TIME

NOTES

WORKOUT *Log*

DATE: S M T W T F S   **INTENSITY**

TODAY'S GOAL

STARTING WEIGHT
GOAL WEIGHT
CURRENT WEIGHT
WATER
💧💧💧💧💧💧💧💧

WEIGHTS

EXERCISE	WEIGHT	SETS	REPS	TIME

CARDIO

EXERCISE	DISTANCE	SETS	REPS	TIME

NOTES

WORKOUT *Log*

DATE: S M T W T F S   **INTENSITY**

TODAY'S GOAL

STARTING WEIGHT

GOAL WEIGHT

CURRENT WEIGHT

WATER

WEIGHTS

EXERCISE	WEIGHT	SETS	REPS	TIME

CARDIO

EXERCISE	DISTANCE	SETS	REPS	TIME

NOTES

WORKOUT *Log*

DATE: S M T W T F S

INTENSITY

TODAY'S GOAL

STARTING WEIGHT
GOAL WEIGHT
CURRENT WEIGHT
WATER
◊ ◊ ◊ ◊ ◊ ◊ ◊ ◊

WEIGHTS

EXERCISE	WEIGHT	SETS	REPS	TIME

CARDIO

EXERCISE	DISTANCE	SETS	REPS	TIME

NOTES

WORKOUT *Log*

DATE: S M T W T F S   **INTENSITY**

TODAY'S GOAL

STARTING WEIGHT

GOAL WEIGHT

CURRENT WEIGHT

WATER
◊ ◊ ◊ ◊ ◊ ◊ ◊ ◊

WEIGHTS

EXERCISE	WEIGHT	SETS	REPS	TIME

CARDIO

EXERCISE	DISTANCE	SETS	REPS	TIME

NOTES

WORKOUT *Log*

DATE: S M T W T F S   **INTENSITY**

TODAY'S GOAL

STARTING WEIGHT
GOAL WEIGHT
CURRENT WEIGHT
WATER
💧💧💧💧💧💧💧💧

WEIGHTS

EXERCISE	WEIGHT	SETS	REPS	TIME

CARDIO

EXERCISE	DISTANCE	SETS	REPS	TIME

NOTES

WORKOUT *Log*

DATE: S M T W T F S   **INTENSITY**

TODAY'S GOAL

STARTING WEIGHT

GOAL WEIGHT

CURRENT WEIGHT

WATER

WEIGHTS

EXERCISE	WEIGHT	SETS	REPS	TIME

CARDIO

EXERCISE	DISTANCE	SETS	REPS	TIME

NOTES

WORKOUT *Log*

DATE: **S M T W T F S**

INTENSITY

TODAY'S GOAL

STARTING WEIGHT

GOAL WEIGHT

CURRENT WEIGHT

WATER

◊ ◊ ◊ ◊ ◊ ◊ ◊ ◊

WEIGHTS

EXERCISE	WEIGHT	SETS	REPS	TIME

CARDIO

EXERCISE	DISTANCE	SETS	REPS	TIME

NOTES

WORKOUT *Log*

DATE: S M T W T F S   **INTENSITY**

TODAY'S GOAL

STARTING WEIGHT

GOAL WEIGHT

CURRENT WEIGHT

WATER

WEIGHTS

EXERCISE	WEIGHT	SETS	REPS	TIME

CARDIO

EXERCISE	DISTANCE	SETS	REPS	TIME

NOTES

WORKOUT *Log*

DATE: S M T W T F S

INTENSITY

TODAY'S GOAL

STARTING WEIGHT

GOAL WEIGHT

CURRENT WEIGHT

WATER

💧💧💧💧💧💧💧💧

WEIGHTS

EXERCISE	WEIGHT	SETS	REPS	TIME

CARDIO

EXERCISE	DISTANCE	SETS	REPS	TIME

NOTES

WORKOUT *Log*

DATE: S M T W T F S

INTENSITY

TODAY'S GOAL

STARTING WEIGHT

GOAL WEIGHT

CURRENT WEIGHT

WATER

WEIGHTS

EXERCISE   WEIGHT   SETS   REPS   TIME

CARDIO

EXERCISE   DISTANCE   SETS   REPS   TIME

NOTES

WORKOUT *Log*

DATE: S M T W T F S   INTENSITY

TODAY'S GOAL

_____
_____
_____

STARTING WEIGHT
GOAL WEIGHT
CURRENT WEIGHT
WATER
💧💧💧💧💧💧💧💧

WEIGHTS

EXERCISE	WEIGHT	SETS	REPS	TIME

CARDIO

EXERCISE	DISTANCE	SETS	REPS	TIME

NOTES

_____
_____

WORKOUT *Log*

DATE: S M T W T F S   **INTENSITY**

TODAY'S GOAL

STARTING WEIGHT

GOAL WEIGHT

CURRENT WEIGHT

WATER

WEIGHTS

EXERCISE	WEIGHT	SETS	REPS	TIME

CARDIO

EXERCISE	DISTANCE	SETS	REPS	TIME

NOTES

WORKOUT *Log*

DATE: S M T W T F S

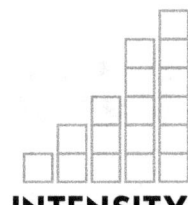
INTENSITY

TODAY'S GOAL

STARTING WEIGHT

GOAL WEIGHT

CURRENT WEIGHT

WATER

○ ○ ○ ○ ○ ○ ○ ○

WEIGHTS

EXERCISE   WEIGHT   SETS   REPS   TIME

CARDIO

EXERCISE   DISTANCE   SETS   REPS   TIME

NOTES

WORKOUT *Log*

DATE: S M T W T F S   **INTENSITY**

TODAY'S GOAL

STARTING WEIGHT

GOAL WEIGHT

CURRENT WEIGHT

WATER

WEIGHTS

EXERCISE	WEIGHT	SETS	REPS	TIME

CARDIO

EXERCISE	DISTANCE	SETS	REPS	TIME

NOTES

WORKOUT *Log*

DATE: S M T W T F S

INTENSITY

TODAY'S GOAL

_____
_____

STARTING WEIGHT _____
GOAL WEIGHT _____
CURRENT WEIGHT _____
WATER
◊ ◊ ◊ ◊ ◊ ◊ ◊ ◊

WEIGHTS

EXERCISE	WEIGHT	SETS	REPS	TIME

CARDIO

EXERCISE	DISTANCE	SETS	REPS	TIME

NOTES

_____
_____

WORKOUT *Log*

DATE: S M T W T F S   **INTENSITY**

TODAY'S GOAL

STARTING WEIGHT

GOAL WEIGHT

CURRENT WEIGHT

WATER

💧💧💧💧💧💧💧💧

WEIGHTS

EXERCISE	WEIGHT	SETS	REPS	TIME

CARDIO

EXERCISE	DISTANCE	SETS	REPS	TIME

NOTES

WORKOUT *Log*

DATE: S M T W T F S

INTENSITY

TODAY'S GOAL

STARTING WEIGHT

GOAL WEIGHT

CURRENT WEIGHT

WATER
💧💧💧💧💧💧💧💧

WEIGHTS

EXERCISE	WEIGHT	SETS	REPS	TIME

CARDIO

EXERCISE	DISTANCE	SETS	REPS	TIME

NOTES

WORKOUT *Log*

DATE: S M T W T F S   **INTENSITY**

TODAY'S GOAL

STARTING WEIGHT

GOAL WEIGHT

CURRENT WEIGHT

WATER

💧💧💧💧💧💧💧💧

WEIGHTS

EXERCISE	WEIGHT	SETS	REPS	TIME

CARDIO

EXERCISE	DISTANCE	SETS	REPS	TIME

NOTES

WORKOUT *Log*

DATE: S M T W T F S

INTENSITY

TODAY'S GOAL

STARTING WEIGHT

GOAL WEIGHT

CURRENT WEIGHT

WATER

WEIGHTS

EXERCISE   WEIGHT   SETS   REPS   TIME

CARDIO

EXERCISE   DISTANCE   SETS   REPS   TIME

NOTES

WORKOUT *Log*

DATE: **S M T W T F S**   **INTENSITY**

TODAY'S GOAL

STARTING WEIGHT

GOAL WEIGHT

CURRENT WEIGHT

WATER
◊ ◊ ◊ ◊ ◊ ◊ ◊ ◊

WEIGHTS

EXERCISE	WEIGHT	SETS	REPS	TIME

CARDIO

EXERCISE	DISTANCE	SETS	REPS	TIME

NOTES

WORKOUT *Log*

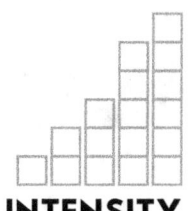

DATE: S M T W T F S   **INTENSITY**

TODAY'S GOAL

STARTING WEIGHT
GOAL WEIGHT
CURRENT WEIGHT
WATER
○ ○ ○ ○ ○ ○ ○ ○

WEIGHTS

EXERCISE   WEIGHT   SETS   REPS   TIME

CARDIO

EXERCISE   DISTANCE   SETS   REPS   TIME

NOTES

WORKOUT *Log*

DATE: S M T W T F S   **INTENSITY**

TODAY'S GOAL

STARTING WEIGHT

GOAL WEIGHT

CURRENT WEIGHT

WATER

💧💧💧💧💧💧💧💧

WEIGHTS

EXERCISE	WEIGHT	SETS	REPS	TIME

CARDIO

EXERCISE	DISTANCE	SETS	REPS	TIME

NOTES

WORKOUT *Log*

DATE: S M T W T F S

INTENSITY

TODAY'S GOAL

STARTING WEIGHT
GOAL WEIGHT
CURRENT WEIGHT
WATER
⬭ ⬭ ⬭ ⬭ ⬭ ⬭ ⬭ ⬭

WEIGHTS

EXERCISE	WEIGHT	SETS	REPS	TIME

CARDIO

EXERCISE	DISTANCE	SETS	REPS	TIME

NOTES

WORKOUT *Log*

DATE: S M T W T F S   INTENSITY

TODAY'S GOAL

STARTING WEIGHT

GOAL WEIGHT

CURRENT WEIGHT

WATER
◊ ◊ ◊ ◊ ◊ ◊ ◊ ◊

WEIGHTS

EXERCISE	WEIGHT	SETS	REPS	TIME

CARDIO

EXERCISE	DISTANCE	SETS	REPS	TIME

NOTES

WORKOUT *Log*

DATE: S M T W T F S

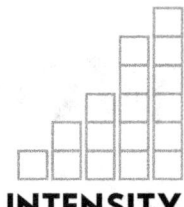
INTENSITY

TODAY'S GOAL

_____
_____

STARTING WEIGHT _____
GOAL WEIGHT _____
CURRENT WEIGHT _____
WATER 💧💧💧💧💧💧💧💧

WEIGHTS

EXERCISE	WEIGHT	SETS	REPS	TIME

CARDIO

EXERCISE	DISTANCE	SETS	REPS	TIME

NOTES

_____
_____

WORKOUT *Log*

DATE: S M T W T F S   **INTENSITY**

TODAY'S GOAL

STARTING WEIGHT

GOAL WEIGHT

CURRENT WEIGHT

WATER

WEIGHTS

EXERCISE	WEIGHT	SETS	REPS	TIME

CARDIO

EXERCISE	DISTANCE	SETS	REPS	TIME

NOTES

WORKOUT *Log*

DATE: S M T W T F S

INTENSITY

TODAY'S GOAL

___

STARTING WEIGHT
GOAL WEIGHT
CURRENT WEIGHT
WATER
💧💧💧💧💧💧💧💧

WEIGHTS

EXERCISE	WEIGHT	SETS	REPS	TIME

CARDIO

EXERCISE	DISTANCE	SETS	REPS	TIME

NOTES

___

WORKOUT *Log*

DATE: S M T W T F S

INTENSITY

TODAY'S GOAL

STARTING WEIGHT

GOAL WEIGHT

CURRENT WEIGHT

WATER
💧💧💧💧💧💧💧💧

WEIGHTS

EXERCISE	WEIGHT	SETS	REPS	TIME

CARDIO

EXERCISE	DISTANCE	SETS	REPS	TIME

NOTES

WORKOUT *Log*

DATE: S M T W T F S   

INTENSITY

TODAY'S GOAL

STARTING WEIGHT
GOAL WEIGHT
CURRENT WEIGHT
WATER
○ ○ ○ ○ ○ ○ ○ ○

WEIGHTS

EXERCISE	WEIGHT	SETS	REPS	TIME

CARDIO

EXERCISE	DISTANCE	SETS	REPS	TIME

NOTES

WORKOUT *Log*

DATE: S M T W T F S   INTENSITY

TODAY'S GOAL

STARTING WEIGHT
GOAL WEIGHT
CURRENT WEIGHT
WATER
💧💧💧💧💧💧💧💧

WEIGHTS

EXERCISE   WEIGHT   SETS   REPS   TIME

CARDIO

EXERCISE   DISTANCE   SETS   REPS   TIME

NOTES

WORKOUT *Log*

INTENSITY

DATE: S M T W T F S

TODAY'S GOAL

STARTING WEIGHT
GOAL WEIGHT
CURRENT WEIGHT
WATER
💧💧💧💧💧💧💧💧

WEIGHTS

EXERCISE	WEIGHT	SETS	REPS	TIME

CARDIO

EXERCISE	DISTANCE	SETS	REPS	TIME

NOTES

WORKOUT *Log*

DATE: S M T W T F S

INTENSITY

TODAY'S GOAL

STARTING WEIGHT

GOAL WEIGHT

CURRENT WEIGHT

WATER
○ ○ ○ ○ ○ ○ ○ ○

WEIGHTS

EXERCISE | WEIGHT | SETS | REPS | TIME

CARDIO

EXERCISE | DISTANCE | SETS | REPS | TIME

NOTES